Manifesting Baby

THE MOTHER'S 30-DAY FERTILITY JOURNAL

SHANNON R RIOS PAULSEN MS LMFT

BEST-SELLING AUTHOR

This book is dedicated to my beautiful son, Elliott Paul Erik. It was written for you and I am eternally grateful you chose me to be your mom. Thank you for making my dream come true. May you manifest all of your dreams in this lifetime. I love you so.

A hundred years from now it will not matter what my bank account was, the sort of house I lived in, or the kind of car I drove...but the world may be different because I was important in the life of a child.

—Forest E. Witcraft, teacher, scholar

TABLE OF CONTENTS

ACKNOWLEDGMENTS

Thank you to my husband, Jonas, for your love and support of my work as an author. I am grateful for your love of our children and for your commitment to being the best partner and parent possible. I thank you for joining me on this journey of partnership, parenthood, and peace.

INTRODUCTION

I f you have picked up this book, you are in the same place I am. You are hoping to bring a baby into the world. This process of fertility can be challenging to say the least. My husband and I have been trying every month for three years to become pregnant. During that time, we adopted our beautiful daughter. When I talk about fertility I am talking about adoption as well. Adoption was a very easy choice for us. Our daughter came to us so quickly. We are currently waiting to adopt a second child (which is taking a lot longer). We still hope to become pregnant. My age? I am forty-five.

This book is meant to be your journal during this time. I also share some of my personal experiences with you during these thirty days. I knew I was meant to write this book for all the mothers also out there forging their way on this challenging path. As I polled my friends and acquaintances, I realized that so many more mothers than we know are silently struggling. This book is meant to be your loving and helpful companion. It is about creating space in your heart and life for your children prior to their arrival. This thirty-day process was truly an intense time for me. And I want you to know I was led to write this book during a particular thirty-day period. I had no idea what these thirty days would bring.

I have journaled my entire life, and I have documented many aspects of this journey of fertility. Yet, this was the only time I wrote for a solid thirty days, calling it specifically "journaling." Researchers have found journaling has many profound benefits, including stress reduction, clarifying thoughts and feelings, knowing yourself better, solving problems more easily, achieving goals, increasing mindfulness, healing, self-confidence, and the list goes on. What better thing to do for yourself during this time?

In the past, I documented my life as a child of divorce (www.healthychildrenofdivorce.com) and my journey to self-love (www.inlovewithme.com), which, by the way, is very related to fertility. I truly thought I would have an easy time becoming pregnant and carrying a healthy baby fullterm; but there were other plans for me: to be a stronger mother. There were also plans for me to assist other "later in life"—or "LIL"—mothers in bringing their children into the world.

My Thoughts on This Journey of Fertility

Our deepest fears and anxieties are manifested through the journey of fertility. These may include fears of being alone, not being loved, being rejected, not being good enough, being flawed, or of being a mother. These real fears can be brought to the forefront as we go through our fertility struggles. My explanation for this is the children we are manifesting want us to do our work PRIOR to their entrance into this physical world. They want you to be able to show them your greatest love possible. If you work through these issues now, prior to their birth, they will have an easier childhood. We all know mothers who did not do their work to heal themselves prior to having children. This creates a challenging path for mothers and their children after they are born. You are manifesting a very wise child—they want you to do the heavy lifting now. They want you to connect with them through this book, before they make their entrance into this world or into your life.

Your process or final method of having a child (an egg donor, adoption, IVF, embryo donation, or natural) does not matter. This book will bring you closer to being the mother you are meant to be. You may even make the conscious choice not to be a mother to a child right now.

About the Book

This book initially felt like "in thirty days the baby will arrive" for me, since we are in the adoption process. But as I journeyed through writing it, I realized it was about clearing the space for this next special child, no matter when or how they arrive.

This journey can be a lonely one. I knew all of you were with me as I wrote this and now you will feel my presence with you over the next thirty days. Even though I am writing another fertility book right now, it was a very strong message that this thirty-day structure was important and this book would come first.

This book is a combination of divine guidance that came to me during these thirty days and my journal entries. I was divinely guided (by my own children, I believe) to write this book for thirty days for myself and other mothers-to-be. I did not censor what showed up, so you will see me pure, raw, and simple. It is messy at times, but I stuck with it through the thirty days. Some days I write about my personal journey and some days I was simply given a meditation. It was truly my sacred path for the thirty days of this fertility journey. No matter what showed up for me personally, meditations always appeared in my journaling. They assisted me each day and I believe in my heart they appeared to assist you as well.

Your own sacred process will emerge from the meditations, questions, and thoughts in the book. It will also emerge as you journal. It is crucial to commit to this for a solid thirty days. You can use my thoughts, questions, and meditations to jumpstart your writing, but the writing you do each day (possibly only free-form some days) will be your own decision based on your situation. This process of fertility is a creative process. Have this journal (or purchase a separate blank journal) by your bed and write in it every night or day.

About the Children

The beautiful souls of all our babies are with us. I feel they are all here with me as I am writing this book. I see my kids along with all the other beautiful souls who are waiting for you to connect with them and become their mothers. My daughter, Emma Emaya, is also here to help us (as you will see from some of my journal entries). Together we are here to help unite mothers with their babies on a soul-to-soul level. I believe my children are creatives and their work begins now before they are on our physical plane. The beautiful news (that I realized through the process of writing this book) is we have more time with our children when we prepare like this, because we can connect with them prior to their physical appearance on earth. This feels like an extra ten to twenty years. Our journey with our children (before they are born and after they are born) is a healing, teaching, and magical one that I am so grateful for.

One more note: If you are reading this book and your deep desire is to be a mother, you WILL be a mother or a mother again. It may not seem to be perfect timing for your mind, but you will be. I know this. This is true for you and for me.

About Me

Know that I hold each of you deeply in my heart. I am here with you on this journey of divine love that can sometimes feel so crazy and lonely. I know I am here to assist mothers in realizing their dreams. I do this through my books, coaching, and retreats. There are so many beautiful soul babies out there waiting for all of you to become their mothers. It is my complete honor to join you and your child in this journey.

In Peace and Love,

Shannon R Rios Paulsen MS LMFT
www.manifestingbaby.com
www.inlovewithme.com
www.healthychildrenofdivorce.com

MOTHER'S MEDITATION

See yourself sitting in a huge circle of mothers-to-be all over the world; mothers who are hoping for a child through adoption or pregnancy. Envision yourself looking into the eyes of all of these beautiful women.

Look around. Take a deep breath and connect to these beautiful women.

They are just like you, hoping, dreaming, wanting, and sometimes feeling defeated. See their strength. Now envision yourself taking the hand of the woman sitting to each side of you. The entire circle of mothers-to-be is holding hands all over the world. Hold your hands as if another mother's hands are in both of your hands. Breathe deeply into this. Feel the love of all these other mothers who are struggling. You are all sending love to each other. Now look deeply into their eyes and say to them, "We've got this. We can do this together."

Breathe into your heart.

CONNECT TO YOUR CHILD

SHARING MY JOURNEY

Thank You from My Heart

I am so glad you are here. I am so grateful to be on this journey with you. I thank you for taking a risk and for daring to look at what could be standing in the way of you and your beautiful baby. Just as the journey of self-love (which I have written about as well) did not feel easy, neither does the journey of fertility. We all know it feels like everyone else easily and effortlessly gets pregnant in the blink of an eye. As I am writing this, another friend of mine announced her second pregnancy in her forties.

I believe we are blessed with this special journey of fertility to allow ourselves to have a more beautiful and easy path with our children once they are born. Doing this work now will provide you with so much prior to and after the arrival of your child. It will allow you to know your strength as a mother before your children arrive. This book will also give you a positive focus for the next thirty days because as we know, this journey does not always have a positive focus, especially if we are working with the medical community to become pregnant.

This is a book of hope and love; it will help you to explore what it means to you to be a mother. You will look at what it means to face the fears all mothers face at some point. You will also consider what it means to potentially share this journey with another person: your partner.

MEDITATION

Say to your future child:

Dear Child/ren, I know you are here. I would not yearn for you if you weren't. Know that I completely and fully support your divine entrance into this world, in your own time, and in your own way. I know it will be perfect. I release all control. I fully open my heart and soul to your divine heart and soul.

Place your hands on your ovaries and see your beautiful eggs (do this regardless of how you will bring your baby into the world). Send them love, health, and strength. See them growing strong; see your beautiful baby inside you. This magnificent soul has chosen you to be its infinite mother. I fully believe that no matter how your child reaches you or at what age they are when they reach you, you were always destined to be their mother.

Connect to the wisdom of your child. What is their message to you?

_____

_____

_____

PARTNERSHIP AND HOLDING SPACE

SHARING MY JOURNEY

I am very angry with my husband today as he has been sick and not interested in making love throughout my entire fertile window. Are you kidding me? Denying a forty-five-year-old woman at such a time is like waiting an eternity to her!

So, I forgave him and know this child is arriving soon.

Holding the Space

You are simply holding space for this magnificent child to arrive. This is not about you, except that you will hopefully become healthier through this process. Perhaps you truly needed this time to get healthier. This child is your divine catalyst for love (and love of yourself).

This is about holding sacred space for this child to show up into. You are merely a vessel for this miracle called life.

Allow yourself to let go of any attachment to this situation and see that you are merely the person chosen to hold space. Let go of all the other pressures you are putting on yourself and your partner.

MEDITATION

Hold your arms out, palms face up. Breathe deeply. What space are you holding for this child now? What do they need from you? What space are you holding for their entire life?

_____

_____

_____

What space will you hold for your partner?

_____

_____

_____

What aspect of this journey do you need to forgive your partner (or lack of a partner) for right now? Who else do you need to forgive around this journey (this could even be yourself)? Let go and forgive.

_____

_____

_____

Is there any part of you that needs to forgive your child for not showing up in your timeframe?

_____

_____

_____

TRUST AND ALLOW LOVE

SHARING MY JOURNEY

Today I realized when I met my husband at age thirty-nine, I had finally come to a place in my life where I truly believed that one day I would have a healthy relationship. I finally had (through my own journey of self-love) a deep trust of the Universe. I was no longer afraid partnership would not happen for me in this lifetime. My husband then appeared at a small restaurant in Thailand. Today, I asked myself, "Do I fully believe I will manifest a baby into this world?"

Preparing for the Worst

When I was younger, I was always preparing in my mind for the worst to happen because I did not want to be let down. I remember doing this, for example, about family trips I was really excited about. I believe I did this because many times, due to the volatile nature of my parents' marriage, I never knew what could happen. Preparing for the worst seems like a strange thing to do but I believe many of us do this for different reasons. I would always say to myself, "Oh, this [what I really want] probably won't happen"—even though, deep down, I really wanted it to happen. I believe that if we carry this pattern into adulthood, it can undermine what we are here to manifest. If we believe we may fail, we just may.

When I reflected on this, I realized that when I was four and my cousin died at seven months in utero, it may have contributed to this pattern of "not getting my hopes up." My aunt lived with us and I can't describe how excited I was for a new sister (especially since I was an only child until I was eleven). And then how very disappointed I was that the baby never came home to play with me. I believe I subconsciously linked this past situation of my cousin dying to my own miscarriage. Before my miscarriage, I was so sure I would become pregnant and carry a healthy baby. Because having a miscarriage was so difficult, I may have said to myself mentally, "I don't get to have that." This old habit from those days as a disappointed child showed up after my miscarriage.

When I reflected further, I knew I had to accept that I do get to have another adoption/pregnancy. I truly deserve this and it will happen. I deserve abundance and joy in this lifetime. I deserve the best.

This baby once again has helped me to remove a huge barrier and allow me to live my magical life (an intention I created with my coach many months ago around fertility).

This also relates to me allowing my relationship with my husband to be happy and successful. I deserve this too, and do not have to live in the fear of failure. I live in the expectation of success. I receive blessings.

MEDITATION

Do you fully believe you will manifest this baby?

What is blocking you from believing in this 100 percent?

_____

_____

_____

Close your eyes. See a door in front of you.

This door is locked. Breathe deeply.

On the other side of this door, your child is waiting for you. You can hear their cry. What do you need to do to unlock this door? Look around you to find the key.

What symbolically is the key to this door? What do you need to do to unlock this door for good and reach your children? What do you know you need to do to open this door wide for your children with your current partner or in your current partner situation?

_____

_____

_____

Close your eyes and say the following:

I believe in my heart that I will manifest this baby or babies.

Take two deep breaths.

Place your hands on your womb and hold the baby/babies in your womb energetically.

Now see your baby/babies running to you. Pick them up and feel their love.

Take two deep breaths.

Ask your baby/babies if there is anything they want to tell you.

_____

_____

_____

SELF-LOVE AND PARTNERSHIP

SHARING MY JOURNEY

I am honestly having a very challenging time with my partner. It seems every time I want to be intimate he creates an issue we need to argue about. I am truly angry with him because during my fertile time he was too sick to try. This still makes me so angry! Why does he have no idea how important this is to me? He had a simple cold! I feel he will use anything to not be intimate. Am I hormonally balanced right now? Most likely not. Does he care? Absolutely not! He left me at home alone last night after I had been out of town for a work trip. Our daughter was screaming, and he just left. Yes, I am beyond frustrated with him. He has not initiated sex in about three weeks. Partners can drive you nuts during this process!

And as I read through this to edit it, I can clearly see I drove him nuts too. But this can be so hard to see at the time.

How do we continue to love ourselves when this process feels so difficult? How do we maintain our balance?

MEDITATION

Close your eyes and ask yourself:

What do I need to do for myself right now?

_____

_____

_____

What do I need to stop seeking from others (especially my partner) and give to myself?

_____

_____

_____

What old patterns do I need to release to bring this baby into the world?

_____

_____

_____

What does my baby need from me?

_____

_____

_____

Who do I need to be each day as a mother right now (how can you act as if you are already this baby's mother)?

_____

_____

_____

ACCEPT SUPPORT

SHARING MY JOURNEY

My truth is that because I am in my forties, I do not feel supported by my family in having children. That sucks. I can't share this dream fully with them. Even three years ago when I told my mom we had fertility issues, her response was, "Oh well, that is just how it goes." There is no support there and it feels like it is due to my age. I don't want to have to justify what I know is right for me and my children.

Seek support. Craft your team. You need a team to manifest this baby. Who is on yours?

First, let me be your support. I am your cheerleader and I support you 100 percent. Who knew being a cheerleader in high school and college would come in handy now?

I don't give a shit about your age. A friend of a friend of mine is pregnant for *the first time* at fifty-one. She is fine and is about to deliver. Since I wrote this first draft, Hoda Kotb, 52, (Today Show) adopted her baby girl. The whole world has shared in her joy. Get yourself as healthy as possible and bring this child into the world because you want to be with them as long as possible. NO ONE knows the amount of time they will have with their children.

Do your emotional and spiritual work now, before they arrive, so you can be the healthiest mom possible. This will allow your child to have the happiest childhood possible. As a kids' therapist, I know for certain it's those early years that are so crucial for children.

MEDITATION

Who else needs to be on your team? Who will you ask?

_____

_____

_____

In the meantime, don't put your life on hold. What is your passion? Go do that.

_____

_____

_____

Are your own thoughts supportive?

_____

_____

_____

What do you need to believe and tell yourself each day?

_____

_____

_____

CREATE PHYSICAL SPACE

SHARING MY JOURNEY

Today is about creating physical space for your baby. I bought my daughter things for almost a year prior to her arrival. I had a small nursery set up. I remember looking in that room and feeling joy—the kids are coming soon! I have now set up another room for the next baby. We painted it yellow with a sailor theme. I go into that room at night to connect to the baby/babies.

MEDITATION

What have you done in your home to show your baby you are ready? This can simply be one cradle. Or it can be an entire room.

_____

_____

_____

What have you done in your *heart* to show the baby you are ready?

_____

_____

_____

Will you put pictures of you, you and your partner, or your family in the baby space?

_____

_____

_____

What can you do to take the next step to welcome this baby energetically before it arrives?

_____

_____

_____

How does this baby know you are ready to welcome them?

_____

_____

_____

What am I, _____ [insert your name], grateful for about this baby?

_____

_____

_____

FEARS AND FERTILITY

SHARING MY JOURNEY

Today I worked with my coach on some of my deepest stuff. I truly believe this 2016 election in the United States is about allowing all of us to look at our deep shadow side. And fertility has a way of bringing this up for us as mothers as well. Wahoo!

We have tried for three years to become pregnant, every month hoping again and again. What I realized today is that I don't feel like I am enough, and I don't feel appreciated. Especially (sometimes) by my husband! If I believe those things, how can I be a mother?

I looked some more and saw that I think for myself and for many others, fertility issues bring up our deepest stuff. Fertility brings up feelings of inadequacy. Everyone else becomes pregnant and I am not being chosen by my child; therefore, I must be inadequate. After my coaching session, I headed to my yoga class, which is very meditative for me, where I focused on this question: "What is the opposite of inadequate for me?" I heard, "love and powerful." I also believe "chosen" is important. I am chosen to carry this baby, I am powerful enough to have an easy pregnancy, I am chosen by the birth mother and I am powerful enough to easily love and care for two children.

MEDITATION

What is your biggest fear about bringing this baby into the world?

_____

_____

_____

What does "infertile" mean to you?

_____

_____

_____

Realizing that we all are *fertile*, what does fertile mean to you?

_____

_____

_____

You must feed and water your soul. Think about caring for you, the beautiful flower. See yourself pick up a fertile flower pot with beautiful flowers.

What do you see when you think about caring for you, the beautiful flower?

_____

_____

_____

What does your soul need to be fertile, right now without a child?

_____

_____

_____

Say to yourself, "I am grateful I am fertile."

_____

_____

_____

We are all fertile. Sometimes it just takes some focused feeding and caring.

TRUST

SHARING MY JOURNEY

As I was doing this thirty-day manifesting book, I went to write down my intention for this next baby in a special children's Bible that I have had since I was a baby. This Bible is a place where I have written a few select requests of God and the Angels over the years. I asked for a brother or sister when I was an only child at eight years old and my mom ended up having two more children by the time I was thirteen!

As I opened this sacred Bible, I saw I had asked for a child before. On April 30, 2014, I asked for my baby to be conceived. I had no recollection of even asking for this, because once I make a request, I put the Bible away. I thought about this and looked up a conception calendar online based on my daughter's birthday of January 17, 2015. It was clear she had been conceived during the time I had asked for this conception. I was blown away. As I am writing this, my eyes are welling up with tears.

I TRUST

I trust I will carry a healthy pregnancy and we will adopt a healthy child. When you fully trust, you let go of the anxiety you have been holding. This old anxiety actually pushes away your dreams. Letting go of it frees your body and soul up to allow your ultimate life path to unfold.

MEDITATION

What will it take for you to fully trust?

_____

_____

_____

Can you completely give your trust to your Higher Power?

_____

_____

_____

I trust because:

_____

_____

_____

Lie down.

Breathe deeply.

Allow the word _trust_ to envelope your entire body. Say to yourself "I trust." Allow all stress to be dissipated by this wonderful feeling of trust in your body. Continue to deeply breathe into this loving space of trust. Ask yourself: "What do I trust?"

_____

_____

_____

Find a sacred place to write down what you want and then let it go fully and trust. Write it down here if you want to.

_____

_____

_____

PATIENCE, FEAR, AND FAMILY

SHARING MY JOURNEY

P*atience* is what these children are teaching us. This is good news because we will need lots of patience as parents.

We just spent twenty-four hours traveling to my husband's family in Sweden. On one flight, our eighteen-month-old screamed and cried for about two hours of the two-and-a-half-hour trip. It was 4:30 AM for her and she had not slept yet. To say my patience was tested is an understatement.

Our children simply trigger our old issues (sometimes even before they are born). They are not the cause of our stress/worry/anxiety. We are! Every time we feel stressed by our children, we must look deeper at our own issues. This is called present-moment or conscious parenting.

MEDITATION

Now ask yourself: What is your *deepest* worry? Your deepest worry is the clue to your deepest gift your children will give you.

_____

_____

_____

How does this deepest worry relate to your own parents?

_____

_____

_____

What do you need to do to release any fears that may be originating from your parents or being raised by your parents?

_____

_____

_____

Forgive your parents for anything you may need to forgive them for. This opens up space for your child or children. What do you need to forgive your parents for?

_____

_____

_____

Now simply release yourself from your parents so you can be you. Think of the good stuff about your parents. Then let everything else fall away. See yourself in a glass container without any negative imprints from your parents. Let go. List the good things about your parents.

_____

_____

_____

Let's ask your child or children, "What is the biggest thing you are teaching me right now through this stress?" Is it to believe? To let go? To be love? To live in euphoria? To simply breathe and relax now? What else?

_____

_____

_____

CONNECTION

SHARING MY JOURNEY

Today has been a tough day. I got my time of the month after two rounds of fertility medications for the last two months. No matter what anyone says, fertility medications are challenging to the body. This period is so bad, and my body feels absolutely horrible and inflamed. I am in a lot of pain. I feel extremely frustrated with my partner during these times as I don't feel he understands what I am going through or how the drugs I have taken to try to be pregnant really make me feel. During this time, I need to connect to myself and take care of myself. I also need to be sure I am connecting to others.

Your connection to your partner and to yourself on this journey are critical. If you are single, connect to those who will support you physically, emotionally, and spiritually. This child wants connected and loving souls to usher them into this world.

MEDITATION

What do you need to do to connect to and take care of yourself during this time?

_____

_____

_____

Close your eyes and ask:

What can I do to positively connect with my partner or other people in my life?

_____

_____

_____

What annoying thing do they do that I can stop focusing on?

_____

_____

_____

What truly is great about them?

_____

_____

_____

How can I be empowered and loving around my partner/others?

_____

_____

_____

Now envision a brand-new start line; commit to the fact that the past is the past. How will you now behave differently with your partner? How will you connect positively with them? How can you give them your unconditional love?

_____

_____

_____

You are creating a new life with your partner and your child. Write down how that new life will look and how you will feel when you are deeply connected.

_____

_____

_____

Day 11

HOLDING YOUR CHILD AND YOUR BOUNDARIES

SHARING MY JOURNEY

Today is about holding your child or children in your heart and body. You can absolutely connect with your children that have yet to be born, conceived, or whom you have not met yet.

A few days before our three-week trip to Sweden, I had a lot of anxiety. I sat in our future baby's room, meditated about this, and really felt it was because I felt like I was leaving our future adopted child and my dream behind in the U.S. Especially when you are hoping to adopt, you wonder about setting up vacations and the possibility that you would be chosen during those times. We were going for three long weeks. In some way, leaving for three weeks did not feel right. I then realized that I could energetically bring this child wherever I go.

Today I am dealing with the sadness of my time of the month. My husband wanted to drive four hours round-trip (after we just arrived in Sweden, jetlagged and with an eighteen-month-old) to see his friend whose wife is eight months pregnant. I told him no bone in my body wanted to go. I took a bath and realized why. I just could not do it today, mentally. It is okay to set your boundaries. Saying no to this was truly taking care of me. Today was not the day for me to go. As I soaked in the bath, I imagined I was pregnant with our adopted baby. I will use that idea (of envisioning me being pregnant with our adopted baby) when I see this woman and another pregnant friend later in this trip.

I have been holding my next adopted child in my womb. When I found out about Emma Emaya, I held her energetically at night and rocked her. For this adoption, I have been doing this before even "knowing" about the new baby that will join us.

MEDITATION

How can you energetically connect with and hold your child?

_____

_____

_____

Where, what, or whom do you need to say no to?

_____

_____

_____

Where do you need to set a boundary so this baby can be birthed into the world?

_____

_____

_____

Close your eyes.

Take a deep breath.

Invite your child in right now.

Feel their loving energy.

Envision your heart opening wide.

Outstretch your hands to your child.

Listen for anything they have to say. What do they want to tell you about their arrival?

_____

_____

_____

Breathe deeply into the love you already feel for them.

Tell them how much you love them, and tell them how deeply you miss them.

Tell them how happy you will be to see them in physical form.

Envision yourself giving them a loving hug.

Breathe deeply.

See them sleeping in their bed in your home. Your precious baby is sleeping peacefully.

Feel the gratitude.

Feel the deep love and trust.

Day 12

BELIEVE AND ENJOY LIFE

SHARING MY JOURNEY

We packed up from the family farm and headed to the coast of Sweden. We were lucky enough to see the sun and it brought such joy! Seeing the sun is an anomaly where my husband is from.

Tonight, as I watched TV (on the one English channel) there was a documentary that featured the band Journey and their song "Don't Stop Believing" from 1983. I just realized my sisters were born during that timeframe (1982 and 1984) and I had also asked for them in my special Bible!

I had previously known *that* song would be a part of my programs for fertility—one day a few months ago those words (don't stop believing) appeared in my mind as a sign to me from the kids. Being a small-town girl from Wisconsin whose first love was a city boy from Chicago, I have always felt deeply connected to that song. It now once again returns to my life as a song of hope and peace.

Enjoy your life now. These beautiful children will be attracted to your joy.

MEDITATION

Play or sing the song "Don't Stop Believing" by Journey. You can also play any other song that has this same effect (puts you in a positive/hopeful frame of mind).

What is the message to you from this song?

_____

_____

_____

Imagine that the Universe is conspiring with you to bring your child or children to you. Say to yourself: _The world is on my side; the world believes in my ability to be a mother to this child. I am perfectly taken care of. In the right timing my child will appear. My hope is infinite._

Surround yourself with infinite hope (feel the word _hope_ permeating your body).

What do you need to believe in right now?

_____

_____

_____

What do you need to do to completely enjoy your life day to day and to live in joy?

_____

_____

_____

Now say: _It is done. It is done. It is done._

MESSAGES AND SIGNS

SHARING MY JOURNEY

The thirteenth has always been a lucky number for me since my birthday is on the thirteenth! Today we went to the coast of Sweden to a place called Tylosand; it is a resort area and spa. It is quite famous. Jonas's sister-in-law's family has a small house here that we stayed in for two nights. I feel that our child is sending us strong messages that he is with us. Today as Jonas and I took a beautiful walk along the rocky shores behind the house, there was one lone sailboat out at sea. "I'm Sailing Away" and "Come Sail Away" have been my theme songs for this sweet soul. The baby's room is decorated in an all-sailor theme. I sense so strongly that this is a water baby.

Later in the day, as Jonas played piano at the restaurant, right above him was a huge butterfly painted on the wall outside (you could see it right through the window as he played). The butterfly has always been my symbol for the children. Then one last perfect symbol showed up while I was at this special spa. As I did yoga (in Swedish), the yoga studio windows overlooked the sea. Directly in front of us were two sailboats—symbolizing to me the two beautiful souls that I believe will join us. I have always believed that our loved ones who have crossed over send us signs. I have now come to believe that in this same way, our beautiful soul babies send us signs before they arrive.

MEDITATION

I would like you to begin paying attention to any signs from your child.

Close your eyes and ask, "What signs have you sent me, dear child?"

_____

_____

_____

If signs do come to you and you are unsure of what they mean, know that many times, the symbols will have some previous meaning in your life. Say to your child, "Please allow me to notice what you want me to see."

What does this baby or child want you to know today?

_____

_____

_____

Write down any fears you have and ask the baby any questions you have for them about your fears.

_____

_____

_____

Day 14

WE ALL DO OUR BEST

SHARING MY JOURNEY

Today, as I lie in bed so frustrated with my husband, so many ideas go through my head.

In *Rising Strong,* Brené Brown talks about us doing our best. Her point is one I have already understood and I believe. She says, "We are all doing the best we can." And I always add, "With the skills we have at the time."

Can you believe your partner, or doctor, or whoever has disappointed you, is doing their best?

I always seem to believe my husband could do better. I hold him to a different standard. What if I just accepted him "as is"? And realize there is nothing in him for me to "fix"?

Then I thought, how about accepting *me* "as is"? Do I really do a good job of this?

MEDITATION

Do you believe you are doing your best in this fertility journey?

_____

_____

_____

What if you truly, deeply accepted yourself "as is"?

_____

_____

_____

As a kid, I always felt pushed by my parents (all with the best of intentions) and now I push myself.

Where are you pushing yourself too hard in this fertility journey?

_____

_____

_____

What can you do to love _you_ more through this journey?

_____

_____

_____

What do you need to let go of?

_____

_____

_____

Always remember: _You are perfect as you are._

Day 15

LIFE THEMES

SHARING MY JOURNEY

As a child, I did not feel safe. Many things happened that created my unsafe story: abuse, two baby cousins passing away, being held up at gunpoint at fifteen years old in my family's convenience store (alone), being hit by a car at twenty years old and seeing it coming, and my childhood home being destroyed by a tornado when I was twenty-one. Writing this, I realize how I was always kept safe. However, I have held a lot of emotion and pain in my body from these events in my life. If we are too tight from past emotions and pain, we don't have room to allow another beautiful soul into our body/life.

In reflecting on these events in my life, I believe it is my life journey (a life lesson in a sense) to feel safe. I was continuously attracted to unsafe situations because I did not feel safe. These situations were part of my life path, as this was obviously an area I needed to focus on in this life—knowing I am safe.

Live your life in freedom today. Enjoy each moment and know you are safe (or that you can get yourself safe if you feel in harm's way). You will have so much space in your life if you live from a foundation of safety. Safety provides a sacred space.

MEDITATION

Look at your life and focus on the big events. What would you say is your life theme?

_____

_____

_____

How could this be related to you becoming a mother?

_____

_____

_____

Are there any recurring life messages that you need to let go of before your child can show up?

_____

_____

_____

Day 16

SAFETY AND OTHERS

SHARING MY JOURNEY

As I write this Donald Trump is the Republican Party's nominee for president. I can truthfully say that a year ago, I felt I could not trust Hillary Clinton. However, I have decided that for some reason I don't feel safe with Trump. To me, this is very critical. Safety is at the core of everything.

MEDITATION

Do you feel safe?

_____

_____

_____

Are you a safe place for a baby to come to?

_____

_____

_____

What is necessary for your baby to feel safe with you?

_____

_____

_____

What can you do to feel safer in your life?

_____

_____

_____

What can you do to help your partner feel safe, loved, and nurtured with you?

_____

_____

_____

Ask your child now, "What do you need from me to feel more safe?"

_____

_____

_____

Close your eyes and see the sacred space of safety surrounding you. Put your hands over your womb, and breathe in safety. As you do this say to yourself, *I am safe, we are safe*. Feel safety surrounding you. Accept this truth—you are safe. Your baby will be safe.

Now envision all the other mothers in this process and send love and safety out from your heart to theirs.

LATER-IN-LIFE MOM (LIL MOM)

SHARING MY JOURNEY

Last night as I was talking with some of my husband's friends here in Sweden about adopting again I got the dreaded question, *"How old are you?"* Really, why do people even have to ask, especially when all you feel is judgment? What is the point? And of course, this question came right after another friend mentioned we were hoping to adopt again. For the record, I would never have told this person we were hoping to adopt again. The small town my husband comes from in Sweden is just that, a small town, and people are nosey! I have been asked this question the last two times I have been in Sweden. So, truth be told, I told her forty-four when I am really forty-five. I should have told her, "Forty-six…and we are trying to have a baby too!" Which we are!

What does it really matter? She has had her own challenges around motherhood. Maybe I should have asked her about that?

As you can see, this situation triggered me. So, I looked deeper. The truth is sometimes, I question if it is OK to be seeking this at forty-five. I sure do feel the judgment from others. I have always wanted to be the best mom possible and truthfully, I know that is why I waited. Now I have guilt about waiting! I have guilt that I won't have as much time with my kids and I have guilt that I am older and my kids may have to deal with that.

I realized when I was recently with my ninety-two-year-old grandma that my kids will be my age when I am ninety-two. That was a reality check in my mind. It's like a generation was skipped.

MEDITATION

Why is it okay for you to adopt/have a baby at _____ (insert your age)?

_____

_____

_____

What is your special commitment to your child since you are an "older, wiser mom"?

_____

_____

_____

How will you take care of your health?

_____

_____

_____

What do you need to do to fully release this concern about your age?

_____

_____

_____

Open your arms and see your children running to you. Scoop them up, hug them and hold them.

Ask them now, "Is it okay with you that I am an older mother?" Listen for what they have to say.

_____

_____

_____

Say to yourself:

This is the time it happened for me; that makes it the right time. I know I have so many gifts to share as a mother and I can give my kids so much in the next twenty years that they are in my care. This first twenty years is the most critical time for children. My commitment is to love, magic, peace, and thriving. My commitment is to live in gratitude every day for my children. My commitment is to balance my life and take time for me. I release all connection to the collective consciousness about age and parenting. I believe older parents can give children easier lives with more wisdom. I release attachments to any age-related guilt, fear, and shame. This time is perfect for me AND my children. I welcome them with open arms. This is perfect timing; I am healthier now than when I was younger. We will have a much easier and healthier life at this point together. It is the quality, not the quantity of time. This is what is true.

I release all and any fear I have carried about getting older and time running out. My time has just begun, and my children know this. Our life together will be magical. Our journey is infinite. It begins long before they are born and will continue after I leave this physical plane.

Envision a huge clock that simply says, "You have all the time in the world."

It is perfect timing. Period.

Day 18

GUILT AND MAGIC

SHARING MY JOURNEY

This age thing is a perfect example of how a mother's guilt shows up even before a baby is born. My husband is not bothered a bit about our ages.

It is time to release any guilt that occupies any space in your body. Release this guilt now and for the rest of your children's lives. Let it go because it will simply drain your energy if you hold onto it.

MEDITATION

Put all your guilt about being an older mom (or whatever guilt you have), past, present, and future into a helium balloon. Blow it out of you and into the balloon (physically do this like you are blowing up a balloon). Now, let the balloon with all the guilt in it go. Watch it go up, up, up and away. As you watch it float away, take deep breaths and feel any guilt float away from your body.

Move your body to release any last guilt that lives in your body.

Say: *I release any fear from my body* (move body) *about being an older mother (or any other guilt that I have).*

I will now transform the concept of "older mother" into "magical mother." I am a LIL, magical mother. This is the new term for mothers in their forties and fifties!

Envision and hold your child. Feel the magic you will feel once they are in your arms.

How can you begin to be a magical mother right now?

Day 19

BEARING FRUIT

SHARING MY JOURNEY

It is a very fertile time of year here in Sweden. All the bushes and trees have wonderful fruit on them. There are apples, yellow and purple plums, raspberries, blackberries, and blueberries. There is a succulent plum tree in the backyard; you can reach up for a sweet plum every time you walk into the house.

We recently walked over to see a neighbor who is renovating an old house he bought. He is twenty-nine and his new wife is thirty-six. We spoke about kids. He talked about the kids' rooms and then he said, "If she can bear fruit." He is a funny guy. He brought to my mind that fertility is like bearing fruit.

At any point, did you physically or emotionally shut down your ability to bear fruit? I had been strongly warned by my mom about becoming pregnant as a young girl. Mom told me that being pregnant (with me) when she was young ruined her life. This warning/fear really stuck with me. So much so that I put the first guy I seriously dated, my first sexual partner (at the age of twenty), through hell because I was so freaked out about becoming pregnant. I made us wait a long time and use two forms of protection! I can truly see that my body could have shut down because I was so afraid of this thing called pregnancy. And in retrospect, I have wished we did have children together when I was younger. My mind tells me it would have been easier, but who really knows? I had to go back to that time and forgive myself in order to open that fertile gateway to have children with someone else.

MEDITATION

Do you have any regrets about not bearing fruit earlier in your life?

_____

_____

_____

Was there any reason you may have shut down your ability to bear fruit?

_____

_____

_____

Is there anything you need to forgive yourself or others for? Anything or anyone you need to let go of?

_____

_____

_____

It is very rainy and wet here, producing beautiful fruits. What is your rain?

_____

_____

_____

Feel the rain falling on your head, and relax into this. Feel the raindrops on your face. What is the rain telling you about your fertility?

_____

_____

_____

One thing that feeds your ability to bear fruit is creativity. Where in your life did your creativity stop? Where do you need to allow your creativity in again? What do you need to do to be creative in your life?

_____

_____

_____

What one activity can you commit to that will bring creativity into your life?

_____

_____

_____

PREGNANCY AND POSTPARTUM PREPARATION

SHARING MY JOURNEY

Today is about releasing, allowing, becoming healthy, and preparing for the postpartum period (this is important whether you have a physical birth or choose to adopt).

If you have pain in your body, I believe this may be old pain (emotional/physical) you have stored in your body from the past, when you were not able to express it (as a child or adult).

Check in with your body to see where you have pain. This may even be a pain in your heart. Push into it a little. Know there is something to uncover and let go. Usually it is some sort of old shame or grief.

Releasing this pain now (and doing the exercises and work in this book) makes room for your baby, for your pregnancy to be easier, and for a healthier postpartum experience—including postpartum anxiety and depression.

Many women deal with postpartum issues. We want to be aware of postpartum issues (now and after birth) so we can enjoy our babies once they arrive. I have seen many mothers have a difficult first few months or years with their children if they do not acknowledge and embrace the postpartum period.

Nutrition is also super important during this time (before and after birth) to help us feel more balanced and help regulate our hormones. My commitments during this journey are: decaf green tea each day, lemon water each day, no alcohol (and this is hard to commit to as I am a social drinker), wheat grass juice (or a serving of liquid greens) every day, and lowering my sugar. I have already given up gluten.

MEDITATION

Does your body have any pain anywhere? If yes, breathe into this pain. Ask this pain what it is telling you that you need to let go of.

_____

_____

_____

What can you do to have an easy pregnancy/time before the baby's birth?

_____

_____

_____

What do you know is important regarding nutrition, now and after the baby is born (what do you give up, lower intake of, or add to your diet)?

_____

_____

_____

If you had postpartum issues, why would that be (hormones, life change, any issues not yet dealt with from your past or childhood)?

_____

_____

_____

What can you do now to minimize any impact of these issues?

_____

_____

_____

Who can be your support after the birth/adoption to alert you if they see depression/postpartum symptoms/signs?

_____

_____

_____

What can you do later, once your baby is born?

_____

_____

_____

What support can you set up ahead of time for this (support of others after the birth)?

_____

_____

_____

What do you need to let go of to have an easy postpartum experience?

_____

_____

_____

Envision your experience after your baby is born (see a positive bonding experience with your baby).

_____

_____

_____

Day 21

SUCCESS AND FAILURE

SHARING MY JOURNEY

After a huge argument with my husband, I realized some strange-but-true truths. In Sweden I can't talk to a portion of my husband's family and when everyone speaks Swedish around me it brings up my old fears of rejection and looking dumb. On top of that, people say things to me like, "Just learn it." If it only were that easy! I realized that foreign languages have scared me my whole life. I never had to take one in college. Then my husband started saying things to people like, "She is so hard to teach, and she does not try." This brought up some old shame and memories of pushing myself hard in school to not look dumb. Now that the fear has been uncovered, maybe I will be able to learn other languages!

This is a very vulnerable time. Our old fears will be easily triggered by our fertility journey; this I know for a fact. We put ourselves under so much pressure during this time. These fears will also show up once your child arrives, so the good news is if you work through them now, you and your child will have more fun once they arrive.

MEDITATION

Take time and freeform your answers to these statements and questions. You can also write out the questions below in your dominant hand and using another color marker and sheet of paper, write out your answer in your non-dominant hand. It will seem strange, but this practice can have some very interesting results.

What fear around success and/or failure stands in your way right now? Take five deep breaths as you consider this question. Breathe deeply into your body. Just see what shows up.

_____

_____

_____

What if you could not fail?

_____

_____

_____

Where has your fear of failure been holding you back?

_____

_____

_____

Do you need to ask your family/friends/partner if they will love you even if you don't have a successful pregnancy, adoption, etc.?

_____

_____

_____

Complete the following statements:

I can:

_____

_____

_____

I cannot:

_____

_____

_____

I will love myself even if:

_____

_____

_____

Day 22

PERFECTION

SHARING MY JOURNEY

"Older and wiser mother" is once again showing up for me. I have such a strong desire to get this right. My fear is that this is not the perfect age. My fears are that I am not strong enough, patient enough, or good enough. I waited to be the "perfect" mom and to attract the "perfect" partner—did I wait too long?

MEDITATION

What anxiety/fear do you need to release about being a "perfect" older mother or a "perfect" mother in general?

_____

_____

_____

How is this fear, _____ [insert answer from above], related to you not being pregnant or a mother now?

_____

_____

_____

Say to yourself: _"I release from my body all old fears of having to get it perfect (and whatever your fear was above). Perfect does not exist in the same sense we learned it as children. There is no punishment for not getting it perfect this time. This journey is perfectly imperfect just like me."_

Take a long walk. As you walk, swing your arms and say whatever you need to say to allow you to release this old nonsense that you have been carrying with you (your old fears). Example: swinging your arms and walking you could say, "I release this old fear that I am not strong enough, patient enough, and perfect enough." Now, as you walk, tell yourself whatever you know you need to hear to manifest this baby (pretend you are talking to a friend about the good things you see in them but you are talking to yourself).

Visualize your fears going back into the earth or releasing them kindly back to those who gave them to you.

Let them go. Breathe deeply; make room for all your messy imperfection that is to come during motherhood.

OUR TRIGGERS

SHARING MY JOURNEY

Today is about marriages, partnerships, and children.

I believe (now that we have one daughter) I can see the reason marriages and partnerships seem to fail at a higher rate after children. We are triggered by our spouses/partners due to our fears, anxieties, and shame. Then we add children to this mix, and both parents' old fears and anxieties about life and parenting are triggered by their children. Being triggered by your partner and your children can feel very exhausting and stressful. This extra anxiety once your child is born (and sometimes lack of sleep) allows you and your partner to more easily trigger each other because your stress is already at a higher level.

The only way through this is to:

- Do this work (outlined in this book) prior to your children arriving.

- Be as conscious as you can regarding your triggers surrounding your children and your partner (once your children arrive).

- Enroll your partner into becoming conscious of their triggers if possible.

As you have noticed from my entries, this trip to Sweden has been challenging. Our daughter is at a very challenging stage for both of us due to our histories. Being out of our routine with a toddler in another country is challenging. And as I already shared, the fact that I can't understand or speak the language provides me with a special trigger when I am in Sweden.

I decided to take my own advice and talk to my husband about this trigger phenomenon. During this trip, due to all the above factors, plus my husband not wanting to go back to the U.S. (he has been missing Sweden and not liking his job in the U.S.), we were triggering each other like crazy.

I had the conversation with him about how I thought we were triggering each other. He seemed to listen. Not long after that, he became triggered about something I said, and I pointed that out. It seemed to help. Then, we started discussing me learning Swedish. Once again, he told me he knew best regarding how I should learn the language (repeating him every time). When I tried to tell him how my mind learns, he interrupted and would not listen. I became so angry I just started screaming over him, "Listen to me!" When I was done, he said, "So I guess you were triggered there." It was so funny to hear him say it and acknowledge it, I started to laugh and then I started to cry—deep sobs. These sobs were related to all my own deep fears and shame about failure, especially around learning another language. I had tried to learn Spanish and felt I failed at that. He said, "I knew there was more under this language thing and it was not just about me." Ha, I love my husband (some days).

We have to be able to look at these triggers in relationships. Whatever your biggest "hot buttons" are with your partner, underneath them is your own anxiety and shame. Some of this stuff is buried deeply. The combination of parenting and partnership (and especially fertility challenges) has the uncanny ability to manifest this anxiety and shame. We then blame this on our partners, creating very pressured partnerships that sometimes fail. Be ready because this process (of being parents to these amazing children) begins with this fertility journey. I believe, once again, that these kids are here teaching us before they arrive so that when they arrive it will be easier. And just a warning, be prepared! Your triggers can hit at any point during your child's development. Ours did around eighteen months (it had been relatively easy prior to that).

MEDITATION

The next time your partner says something that triggers you and you feel upset, remember they are triggering old emotions from your past.

Breathe into this emotion and let it move through you.

Ask yourself:

Who did my husband/partner remind me of in this situation?

_____

_____

_____

Why did what they said or did trigger me so much?

_____

_____

_____

Is there any request I need to make of them?

_____

_____

_____

How can I become present when I am triggered (e.g., breathe, walk away, center myself)? What do I need to do when I feel triggered in the future?

_____

_____

_____

REALIZATIONS

SHARING MY JOURNEY

Today is about self-realizations.

You can never achieve perfection. It is all exactly the way it is supposed to be. Your Higher Power is the only entity who knows perfection. Put perfection in those hands.

No matter what comes up for you during this journey, I am here to tell you it is perfect, although it may not be the way you had imagined. I am sharing with you the raw truth of what my husband and I had to go through during this journey. I believe truly wanting to be parents to these children allows you to see some deep stuff between you and your partner. It sure showed up for us during these thirty days!

My husband is not happy with his job in the U.S. and misses his homeland. I believe this comes out in anger towards me as he sees me as the one trapping him in the U.S. Today he told me he is staying in Sweden and I can take our daughter and go home to the U.S. solo. Wow.

During this time in Sweden, I have had a lot of downtime. I have seen a lot about my husband and myself. What I realized about me (I will refrain from sharing what I feel I learned about my husband):

- I wait for the next bad thing from him or I wait for me to do the next bad thing.

- I stay too long and beg him to stay, which never works; he just feels trapped.

- I try to get it all right, to be perfect and ensure that others love me so there is no bad consequence to me.

- The abuse I suffered as a child has made me believe, on some level, I am a bad person. That I will always fuck up and be punished for it. I will do anything not to fuck up (and then it seems I always do). This is true about any of our deep fears; we usually end up manifesting them in our life in some way.

- I have lived in a state of anxiety my entire life. It has driven me. On this trip, I have taken so much downtime that the anxiety is lessening. This anxiety can make me mean and angry with others whenever I think they are rejecting me.

- I have tried my best; I have done well enough. I am so grateful for Emma Emaya.

- I love me and these kids have helped me manifest my best self, even if they may not come into physical form in my life.

- I feel the angels so strongly with me right now.

- I can handle this, I can do this.

- Even though Jonas told me he is staying here, I can go home with Emma Emaya.

- My alone time here has been perfect. I can do this.

MEDITATION

What big realizations have you had about yourself during these past twenty-four days?

_____

_____

_____

How will these realizations allow you to be the best mother possible?

_____

_____

_____

How can you see these children as a gift, no matter what is currently "true" in your life?

_____

_____

_____

Can you see that whatever is happening in your partnership (or in your relationship with others if you don't have a partner), it is important that it happens because the two of you (or you) have to be the strongest parents possible so you can thrive when your children do arrive?

_____

_____

_____

Today, let go of any anxiety about a baby or pregnancy. Breathe into this: *I release all anxiety related to this baby/pregnancy/birth.*

HEALING THROUGH PARTNERSHIP

SHARING MY JOURNEY

Well, by gosh and by golly, we are on the plane (together) going back to the United States. Yesterday, Jonas had informed me he was staying, and Emma and I could go back alone. I had some big emotions. I reached out for support, let Jonas take care of Emma, and I took care of me. I spent time with myself doing my own work and healing (I shared my revelations yesterday). I knew I would need some time with me prior to the twenty-four-hour trip back home if I was to be the only person caring for a nineteen-month-old!

While alone in that dark room in the farmlands of Sweden, I did some EFT (Emotional Freedom Technique) for my own healing and had long discussions with my angels and Higher Power. I decided this time, I would not beg (as I had done in the past), and he would have to make his own choice. I knew Emma and I could be okay. We would need to move to Wisconsin to be closer to family for certain, but we would be okay. I gave up on having any more kids. It was so sad to think about going back to that fully decorated nursery.

Deep down I knew he was very sad to leave his home country. It truly had caused stress our entire trip in Sweden. When he is sad, he sometimes says things he does not truly mean, but I had no choice at the time but to believe him and take care of me. I did not beg him to come back with us. I accepted his choice this time, finally. This was a huge step for me.

Jonas finally decided to take care of himself and he went for a long walk. He came back and apologized.

So, as you see, things can get bad during this process of your fertility/parenting journey. And looking back, I am grateful this happened before we had any more children so we could work through it.

We agreed to go back to the U.S. and to devise a plan to strengthen our relationship. In the end, struggles can bring us closer if we allow that. And, in the meantime, it can feel absolutely horrible.

MEDITATION

If you are currently struggling with your partner or lack of a partner, reflect on this:

What do you need to do to take care of you and love you, since this is all you can ever do?

_____

_____

_____

What time can you take for yourself, alone?

_____

_____

_____

What can you and your partner do to strengthen your relationship?

_____

_____

_____

What conversation could you have with your partner to look deeper, taking responsibility for your role and not make them wrong?

_____

_____

_____

How can this difficult fertility journey bring you closer to your partner and yourself?

_____

_____

_____

If you have a partner, take time to discuss this with them. If you don't have a partner decide who will be your support team/person. Share some of your thoughts and fears with them.

OPEN YOUR HEART

SHARING MY JOURNEY

I had the best conversation ever with Jonas today.

Immediately after we returned from Sweden, we had an appointment to visit a wonderful woman named Susana to do "Bodytalk" together. This is a body therapy that I can't quite explain, but we needed to do something to focus on our relationship. We met with her and it was a profound experience. Jonas looked me in the eyes and we were clear we were going to work together on this relationship. I forgot to mention that before we left the house, we had been really frustrated with each other. He did not do something he had promised he would do. His not keeping his word is a trigger for me. It makes me feel unsafe.

Once we returned home, we sat outside on our beautiful deck in the mountains. I had realized something pretty big: that I shame him when he does not do something he has promised. I shared that with him, and it was not easy to do that. He said, "I know, and I think due to my history, I wait for you to shame me about something." I told him I absolutely did not want to do this any longer. I truly had not been aware of this pattern in our relationship, but it made sense because of my own family history. I then asked him a few questions about why he does not do things he knows he needs to. It was revealing, and he chose to look deep. It was one of our most connected conversations ever.

MEDITATION

Close your eyes and take a deep breath. Feel your body sinking down into wherever you are sitting or lying. Let go of any stress from your body. Now envision your heart, this beautiful heart that gives you life. Feel gratitude for your heart. Place your hand on your heart and feel the steady beat. Breathe into this.

If you are single, look at anyone who sometimes frustrates you (your parents or another significant person in your life). Do this exercise with them.

Ask your heart: What do you want to tell me about this relationship (or lack of relationship)?

_____

_____

_____

How can you open your heart more (share, be vulnerable, be honest) with your partner/ future partner?

_____

_____

_____

What is your role in the frustrations in your relationship?

_____

_____

_____

What areas need to be resolved or moved to the next level in order for you and your partner to provide a loving space for a child? What one step can you take from your heart to move towards that?

_____

_____

_____

In some ways, partnership is a daily decision. What decision will you make from your heart today about your partnership?

_____

_____

_____

Day 27

IVF—I'M VERY FERTILE

SHARING MY JOURNEY

Today I took time for me. I took a long walk and ended up sitting at the edge of a river. All of the possible medical procedures were going through my mind and I was wondering what more we should do or try, if anything. I have a very strong belief in the Universe and Higher Power. I also believe in my power to manifest. I decided to ask the angels for guidance on this very challenging topic of fertility treatments. I realized I can create my own process of universal IVF (for pregnancy and/or adoption). This felt so positive and freeing. I walked away with huge hope in my heart.

MEDITATION

This is a self-IVF meditation to manifest your embryo (and again it does not matter how or at what age your child is when they arrive, this is energetically connecting with them). No matter how your baby gets to you, it can be helpful to envision this process as your process.

Say to yourself: "IVF—*I'm very fertile.*"

Close your eyes, envision your partner (or anyone else), connect to the love you have for them. Feel this love in your heart. Now envision in your mind strong and healthy sperm (your partner's or donor sperm). Connect with them. Thank them for your pregnancy and baby. Connect to the actual sperm that will impregnate your egg. See its strength, health, and determination in your mind as you envision it. Tell it anything it needs to hear.

Envision your strong, beautiful, and healthy egg. It is strong and also willing to allow the sperm to connect with and merge with it.

Now it is time to talk to your egg, the one follicle that will become your baby. Tell her anything you need to let her know right now.

Envision this beautiful sperm meeting this beautiful egg inside of you. Imagine your loving egg has arms and she is fully accepting this sperm.

Take a deep breath.

See them moving down the fallopian tube together and implanting in your fertile uterus. They are so happy there together as your beautiful embryo. This embryo grows into your healthy and happy baby. Envision months one, two, three, four, five, six, seven, eight, nine, and now see your child being born and placed into your loving arms.

DREAMS AND CONNECTION

SHARING MY JOURNEY

I have always heard you should listen to your dreams. I have also heard that when you go through fertility challenges, your dreams may speak to you. I normally have a very hard time remembering my dreams. As it so happens, during this thirty-day period I had some interesting dreams that I actually remembered. This made me realize that a discussion about dreams needs to be in this book.

During these thirty days, I went deep into my own emotions and fears. That was not my intent; it simply happened because of my commitment to write for these thirty days for my child and for your children. It was an intense thirty days. One particular dream was especially intense for me.

In this dream, a man I loved and longed for in the past (an old love) came back into my life again and could not be with me. He left me again.

I took some time to look at this. With what I knew about dream interpretation, I realized I have a pattern of wanting someone to love me, and not feeling loved (I feel this in my relationship with my husband at times as well). Also, I saw the man in this dream as ME not wanting ME. I have heard that the main character in your dreams is truly you.

I then realized the miscarriage I had gone through and the fertility issues are yet another manifestation in my life and mind of me not being "wanted." I took time to ask more questions of myself about this dream. I then saw butterflies—my symbol for my babies. And I realized, you can't "catch" butterflies, they are elusive, just like fertility feels to me. Butterflies have always been symbolic of my babies to me.

I shared these realizations about not feeling wanted with Jonas (which also could originate from being an unplanned pregnancy when my mom was eighteen).

To get more connected with him, I asked Jonas to do a tantric practice with me this morning and he did (with him being Swedish this was big news)! Yes, we got naked and looked in each other's eyes. We sat for about twenty minutes and afterward had great sex (which is not all that common for us)! Sex is not the goal, but it simply happened. Remember...I am honestly journaling about what showed up during this thirty-day period!

MEDITATION

Do you have any stories that may be holding you back from your connection with your partner and/or your children?

_____

_____

What do you want to do to minimize these stories so that you can strengthen your connections in your life?

_____

_____

What might your dreams be telling you?

_____

_____

Do you have any recurring dreams that may be telling you something?

_____

_____

Keep a blank journal/notebook by your bed. Write down your dreams.

Tantric Practice

Perform this tantric practice with your partner (or envision one if you don't have one, you can also do with a friend).

Get naked (or you may want to do this clothed with a friend).

Sit across from each other (a bed is good, or any other surface).

Grab each other's arms at around the elbow point.

Both of you lean back.

Allow the weight of the other person to support you in leaning back.

Stare directly into each other's eyes (ideally for twenty minutes, but at least ten).

You and your partner will most likely have some reactions as you sit in this somewhat uncomfortable position holding each other up. Remember your reaction to this practice (whatever happens for you or your partner) is a representation of how you react to life.

Think about two questions (each of you can think about these):

How can you support your partner in this fertility journey?

_____

_____

_____

What are you resisting on this journey?

_____

_____

_____

SELF-VALIDATION

SHARING MY JOURNEY

After returning from our long vacation to Sweden, I was booked solid with my corporate coaching clients. In all my conversations, self-validation versus external validation showed up again and again. Every single leader asked, "How do we self-validate?" My response was: You give **yourself** the positive recognition instead of looking for it from someone else. You validate yourself for "being enough and doing enough."

When something shows up so strongly in my coaching, I know I need to look at it deeper in my own life. I decided this must be showing up around motherhood, fertility, and/or partnership for me (because work for me truly is easy and fun).

I asked myself, "What have I done well?" Even though I am not perfect, I am a very connected, loving mother. I have taken this next phase of my fertility journey full on. I am helping myself and other mothers manifest these beautiful souls. This is a priceless gift to mom and baby. I am grateful for my vulnerability in all of this, to bare my heart and soul for the goodness of my children, my partnership, my life, and all the other beautiful baby souls who want their moms to be as healthy as possible before they show up.

MEDITATION

What can you acknowledge yourself for in these areas below? What have you already done well? Write your answers down.

<u>Motherhood:</u>

_____

_____

_____

<u>Fertility:</u>

_____

_____

_____

<u>Partnership:</u>

_____

_____

_____

<u>Career:</u>

_____

_____

_____

<u>Career and Motherhood:</u> Is there anything you want to acknowledge here about slowing down? What do you want to acknowledge about how much time you will spend with your child versus your career? I sense your child really wants you to look at this and discuss this with your partner so you both have the time you need with this beautiful child once they arrive. Write this in the future tense of what you *will* be doing.

_____

_____

_____

THE MIRACLE OF LIFE

SHARING MY JOURNEY

This final day of your journey is about the miracle of life.

As I was finishing up this thirty-day period, I learned a close family friend was tragically killed in a work accident. He was such a kind-hearted family man. I am sad for his beautiful family. He was only sixty-five. Always remember that while our problems seem big, we should be grateful for this life we've been given.

Some messages I heard as I contemplated his passing:

- Practice letting go of the anger and frustration faster.

- Remember to love, love, love.

- Love yourself.

- Love your partner (or future partner).

- Love your baby (even before they arrive).

- Acknowledge all that you are and all that you have done.

- Live from your heart.

- Have gratitude for this moment and the day when you will become a mother, again and again and again until it is a reality.

As I awakened today, I remembered my dream (which again is very unusual for me). It was once again a profound dream.

First there was a snowstorm. Many cars were completely buried in the snow, and some friends and I were walking down one of the blocks filled with parked cars. I happened to see a dog's eyes in one of the cars. My friends and I began to dig. Inside of the car there were three men. The men had no food in their car and they had been afraid they might die in there. I felt deeply connected to one of these men. The men stayed with us after we rescued them. We went to my amazing home on the lakefront (a future goal of mine). As this man and I sat there together, he took my hand. I felt such deep love and knew this was a forever love. It felt warm, cozy, deep, and beautiful.

Upon waking, I wanted to sink back into the beautiful feeling of this yummy love. As I awakened, I realized that this represented me finding *me*, finally. I had finally rescued myself and I was there with me. The dream felt so beautiful, and a perfect ending to this book. I only had one page left in the small journal I had started with, and I was at my thirty-day mark.

I am eternally grateful for this fertility quest. It is like a true vision quest, where you find yourself buried deep in the snow. I made a lot of snow forts and caves as a kid and felt so safe in them. The snow in my dream was symbolic of this feeling of safety as a kid and so was being rescued (as I felt many days I wanted to be rescued from my home environment). And I love, love, love water; I will live on the water one day.

This dream was showing me that I am wanted now by me; there is no more longing. I have rescued me. I am staying with me. I once heard we think, usually subconsciously, that our children will fill something inside of us, and that is why we long to be mothers. After the dream, that old longing for something more was absolutely gone.

Whew…this was a long day. At the end of this thirtieth day, my twenty-month-old and I watched *The Miracle of Life* (she loved it). It is such a beautiful movie showing how we are all connected.

MEDITATION

Take a deep breath and ask yourself:

Where will you find you? Hint: It is not through your partner or children.

_____

_____

_____

How can you fully embrace you?

_____

_____

_____

How can you fully take care of the beautiful child/baby inside of you (that is truly you)?

_____

_____

_____

Watch the movie *Miracle of Life* so you can envision you and your baby being created (http://manifestingbaby.com/miracle-of-life/) and allow yourself to revel in the magic of your life and theirs.

In memory of Craig "Juice" Wirth—may we live with a kind heart towards ourselves, as Craig lived with his heart open to others.

CHILDREN'S MESSAGE OF LOVE

Close your eyes. See all the beautiful children who have helped me write this book.

They are your children. They are powerful. They are waiting for you to clear the space to allow them to pass through you into this lifetime. Breathe into this truth.

Message from the children: *To all our divine mothers. We are so grateful for you. If you have this dream, we are meant to become your reality. We are here. Please connect with us. Begin the relationship with us now, we are here.*

Breathe deeply.

We love you, we support you, and we honor you. Our timing will be perfect; remember this. Receive support on this journey. When you feel defeated, connect to us. Time is something someone made up. We will have all the time in the world together.

Now place yourself back in that circle that we created at the beginning of the book with all the mothers-to-be. See yourself holding hands with all the other mothers in the huge circle.

Feel the loving energy of all the mothers. Now see all the beautiful children standing behind their mothers. Envision your child or children standing behind you. They place their hands on your shoulders.

Feel their strength and love. Breathe into this.

Mom, we love you, we are here, you are not doing this alone. Continue to do your work and make room in your soul for us. We have been here all along. We will meet again soon on the physical plane. We love you, Mom.

Open your arms, palms face up. Feel your child or children holding your hands. Now see them look you in the eyes. *We love you, Mom.*

Listen for any other messages they have for you.

EPILOGUE

As I was completing the final edits of this book, my beautiful son was born into this world. Elliott Paul Erik was born and placed into my arms on April 11, 2017. We were able to be at the hospital for his birth and it was so special. The day we were chosen, the Journey song "Don't Stop Believing" came on the radio. It was a sign from our son and the angels. At his birth my angels (literally) played the harp outside of his room. The harp is my favorite instrument and I had one on the beach at my wedding. The song "Can't Help Falling in Love" by Elvis was playing as he was born. It was simply magical. I am so grateful for this beautiful boy. And I can honestly tell you that I feel so full and complete as a mother. I manifested this beautiful boy into my life. My two children are wonderful. I feel no need for any other children at this point. That could always change but for now, I am grateful for this journey of fertility, adoption, and motherhood. I am complete. Thank you for joining me on this beautiful journey.

ABOUT THE AUTHOR

S hannon Rios Paulsen, MS LMFT is a Professional Coach and Licensed Marriage and Family Therapist who has specialized in families and children for fifteen years. Due to her own fertility journey, she knew she was meant to write a book for other mothers. She coaches and leads retreats for women whose dream is to become mothers later in life (www.manifestingbaby. com).

Shannon has assisted hundreds of families in successfully navigating the divorce and parenting process (www.healthychildrenofdivorce.com). She has also written *In Love With Me: The 10 Strategies for Self-Love and Successful Relationships* http://bit.ly/10stepsselflovebook or (www. inlovewithme.com). She is the author of two best-selling guided meditations: *The Healing Journey Within: Meditations for Abundance and Love, Volume I (Deserving)* http://bit.ly/selflovemedvol1 and *Volume II (Manifesting)* http://bit.ly/selflovemedvol2 as well as the best-selling book, *The 7 Fatal Mistakes Divorced and Separated Parents Make* http://bit.ly/divorceparentbook or (www. healthychildrenofdivorce.com).

Ms. Rios Paulsen lives in the mountains of Colorado with her husband and two children.

Made in the USA
Middletown, DE
27 March 2019